soup

NEW
HOLLAND

contents

introduction

Soup is one of the most basic foods. Its history streches far into the past when soup was simply water simmered with whatever basic ingredients were available for flavour.
Soup then was never about quality ingredients and complex flavours. Rather, it was simply about survival. Yet soup was still a meal shared between family members and acquaintances.

Thick hearty soups are served in the cold months to nourish and satisfy hungry children and to give energy to people at the end of a hectic day. Cold refreshing soups are served in hot weather and humid climates to invigorate and enliven after an exhausting day.

Throughout the Western world soups are served as a teaser to the coming meal, while in China soup is served after a meal as an invigorating finale. In many European countries soup is served between courses to refresh the palate. In fact, soup is served more often and in many more flavour combinations throughout the world than any other meal.

Soups have changed in manyways over the years, with modern cooking methods and ingredients taking over from traditional methods and ingredients. What would Great Grandpa have said if Great Grandma had served him up a soup of onions cooked in white wine and brandy? The very idea! Soups with Japanese liqueur in them. Soups served chilled! Ah yes times have changed.

It could be argued that the level of a nation's culinary sophistication can be seen in the soups it serves. There's nothing wrong with good old traditionals like beef shin or calf's foot, however we tend now to use more modern ingredients.

The modern cook prefers to stay away from the predictable and concentrate on a selection of recipes that use imaginative ingredients in imaginative ways. In the recipe selection offered in these chapters we include, with the traditional, some delightful variations.

When planning your dinner party, choose your soup carefully. A dinner of several courses should be preceded by a light clear soup, preferably a consommé. Thick soups, on the other hand, should be regarded as part of the main meal.

Soups are time-honoured comfort foods, with well-rounded flavours and soothing, sustained warmth. Prepared more often in a single pot, they can incorporate all kinds of ingredients in combinations that are as nutritious as they are delicious.

Be lost in a sense of well-being as the contents of your cooking pot boil and bubble and the tendrils of steam and aroma curl up, permeating the surroundings and inducing a real warmth and homely feeling. What dreary winter afternoon is not brightened by the companionable murmur of a simmering soup on the stove?

A soup can be thick or thin, it can range from a clear, light broth to a hearty chowder almost thick enough to eat with a knife and fork. It has been noted that several centuries ago soup was served over 5 courses as a total meal. This has not been repeated in these modern times to our knowledge.

At the turn of the century it was normal to have soup always be served as part of the evening meal. These days however, we are not as regimented and soup can be served at any time of the night or day and in almost any position on the menu – from snack to main course, from entrée to dessert. Or indeed, soups can and sometimes do constitute an entire meal.

So you will see in these recipes that a soup can be served as a first course or a main course. It can also be a between-meal snack, to satisfy those cheeky customers just home from school or work.

Our selected recipes offer soups of all types for all occasions and are built upon one of the basic stock recipes that appear in this introduction. Most are simple to prepare and in most situations require a minimum investment in time.

Of course, we offer slow-cooked soups as well as some real fast heat and serve varieties, a selection of recipes to suit all appetites and tastes.

TECHNIQUES

While soup is very easy to make and delightfully satisfying to eat, there is no doubt that a few tricks of the trade and some handy hints will give you superior results, even if you have never made a pot of soup before.

COOKWARE

While quality cookware is always a joy to use, remember that soups are centuries old and most of our ancestors didn't have the pleasure of shiny new cookware and elegant stovetops. Just use whatever large saucepans or stockpots you have. If you find you need a new saucepan, purchase a high-quality pot with a strong enamel or non-stick surface, or a stainless steel pot that has an insulated base. Cast iron works well too.

INGREDIENTS

We all want to use the best, freshest ingredients when we prepare foods for our family or friends, and there is no doubt that quality ingredients contribute towards a more delicious and healthy end result. Meat, fish, poultry, spices and herbs should always be in peak condition for the best soups. Vegetables, however, can be a little wilted or past their prime. When you are about to make a soup or stock, clean out your vegetable crisper and see what has been left behind. Of course, common-sense should prevail, so don't use any vegetables that smell unpleasant or are obviously mouldy.

NOTE

Most soups freeze well. When freezing any liquid, leave a 5mm space between the soup and the lid of the container, as liquid expands during freezing.

homemade stocks

FOUNDATIONS OF FLAVOUR

The basis of a quality soup is a quality stock – it's as simple as that! In years past, a good soup always began with hours of simmering simple vegetables and, perhaps, some meat bones to create a rich broth.

These days, however, if you prefer to bypass this step, there are several prepared stocks available from your local supermarket. They can be found in liquid form, as a paste or as a powder.

Generally speaking, it is much easier to purchase liquid stocks as they have a true flavour and are literally ready to use. Pastes are a good option too because they are concentrated, which allows you to add as much water as necessary to dilute the flavour according to your tastes.

In our opinion, most stock powders should be avoided if the liquid or paste stocks are available. These powders are often heavily salted and therefore offer a salty rather than 'true to taste' flavour. The ratio of powder to water can be difficult to master and some brands contain artificial flavours and colours.

By far the most rewarding and delicious stock is the one you make yourself. Contrary to popular belief, stocks are not difficult to make and, although they do need to simmer for quite some time, their preparation time is minimal.

The following recipes will guide you through the basics of making a good stock – regardless of which type of stock you wish to make, you can follow one of these basic methods. If you have any vegetables in your refrigerator that are looking a little wilted and sad, throw these into the stockpot too as they will add extra flavour and colour.

Oh, and one other thing – remember that stocks freeze extremely well for extended periods of time, so don't be afraid to make a pot of stock when you have large amounts of vegetables, roasted meat bones or turkey frames (from the Christmas bird) on hand. Make the stock and pop it in the freezer for your future risotto or soup.

Making good stock is a very simple procedure. The ingredients are simmered in a pot – when strained and degreased the cooking liquid becomes a savoury essence to serve on its own, store for later use, or use in preparing another dish. Recipes for the five basic stocks follow on the next pages. Stock comes from humble beginnings – inexpensive cuts of meat and bones, fish bones and heads, or chicken wings and backs.

Attention to detail will reward you with a rich and tasty stock. All large fat deposits should be removed beforehand, but large bones will give you treasured gelatine, if cracked first, and provide body to your stock.

During cooking, remove scum that occasionally collects on top of the liquid. Scum consist of protein particles released by meat and bones, these float to the surface, where they gather in a foam. As nutritious as it is, the foam must be removed lest it cloud the stock. Skim off the foam as it forms at the start of cooking, skim thereafter only as the recipe directs.

After its initial rapid cooking, stock must not be allowed to return to rapid boil as the turbulence will muddy the liquid. As a final cleansing, the stock should be strained through a fine sieve or a colander lined with muslin.

Rich vegetable stock

MAKES 8 CUPS

1. Wash all the vegetables and slice or chop roughly.
2. Heat the olive oil in a large stockpot and sauté all the vegetables for 20 minutes until they begin to develop a golden colour on the surface.
3. Add the parsley, peppercorns, bay leaves and water to cover (about 4 litres) and bring to the boil. Simmer for 3 hours, skimming the surface to remove any scum that accumulates.
4. Add salt to taste, then simmer for a further few minutes if you would like a more intense flavour. Allow to cool then strain, pressing on the solids. Use within three days or freeze for up to 12 months.

NOTE

In addition to the vegetables above, you can add any other vegetables in your refrigerator that are past their prime – greens, root vegetables, corn and peppers all work well.

2 tablespoons olive oil
1 turnip or swede
5 cloves garlic
3 stalks celery
3 large carrots
10 mushrooms
3 large onions
4 tomatoes
2 leeks, well washed
2 parsnips
10 sprigs parsley
1 teaspoon peppercorns
8 Brussels sprouts
4 bay leaves

Chicken stock

MAKES 10 CUPS

1. Wash all the vegetables and slice or chop roughly.

2. Place all ingredients in a large stockpot. Add water to generously cover the ingredients (about 4 litres). Bring to the boil then simmer for 2–3 hours, skimming the scum off the surface as it rises to the top.

3. Add salt to taste, then strain the stock through a sieve lined with absorbent paper or cheesecloth.

4. Place in a large saucepan and chill until the fat solidifies on the surface. Remove the fat and use or freeze the stock.

2 carrots
4 stalks celery
3 onions
1 leek, chopped
8 sprigs parsley, chopped
4lb 6oz (2kg) chicken frames or
   wings
1 teaspoon peppercorns

Fish stock

MAKES 10 CUPS

17½oz (500g) fish bones, heads
   and trimmings, washed
2 carrots, chopped
4 stalks celery, chopped
3 onions, roughly chopped
8 sprigs parsley, chopped
6 white peppercorns
good pinch of ground nutmeg
1 teaspoon salt

1. Place the fish pieces and 4 cups water into a saucepan and bring to the boil.
2. Skim off any discoloured froth from the top. Add remaining ingredients and simmer gently, uncovered, for a further 30 minutes. If cooked too long the stock becomes bitter.
3. Strain and discard the bones and vegetables. Use the stock within two days or freeze it in a sealed container.

Seafood stock

MAKES 4 CUPS

2lb 4oz (1kg) shrimp (prawn)
shells and heads
2 carrots
4 stalks celery
3 onions
1 leek
8 sprigs parsley, chopped
1 teaspoon peppercorns

1. Thoroughly wash shells and heads.

2. Wash all the vegetables and slice or chop roughly, then place in a large stockpot with the shells, parsley and peppercorns. Cover with cold water (about 4 litres), bring to the boil and simmer for 1–2 hours, skimming the scum off the surface as it rises to the top.

3. Add salt to taste, then strain through a sieve lined with absorbent paper or cheesecloth.

4. Place in a large saucepan and chill until the fat solidifies on the surface. Remove the fat and use or freeze the stock.

Veal stock

MAKES 10 CUPS

1. Fill a large stock pot halfway with water. Bring the water to the boil, add the veal meat and bones, and blanch them for 2 minutes to clean them.

2. Drain the meat and bones in a colander, discard the liquid. Rinse the meat and bones under cold running water and return them to the pot.

3. Wash all the vegetables and slice or chop roughly. Then place in a large stockpot with the veal bones and meat and all remaining ingredients.

4. Cover with cold water (about 4 litres), bring to the boil and simmer for 2–3 hours, skimming the scum off the surface as it rises to the top.

5. Add salt to taste, then strain through a sieve lined with absorbent paper or cheesecloth.

6. Place in a large saucepan and chill until the fat solidifies on the surface. Remove the fat and use or freeze the stock.

2lb 4oz (1kg) veal breast or
veal shin meat, cut into 3in
(75mm) pieces
4lb 6oz (2kg) veal bones
(preferably knuckles), cracked
2 carrots
4 stalks celery
3 onions
4 sprigs fresh thyme, leaves
removed and stalks discarded
3 unpeeled cloves garlic, crushed
8 black peppercorns
1 bay leaf

Brown stock

1. Preheat oven to 420°F (220°C), place meat, bones, carrots, celery and onions in a large roasting pan and roast for about 1 hour, until well browned.

2. Transfer the contents of the roasting pan to a large saucepan. Pour 2 cups of water into the roasting pan and, with a spatula, scrape up all the brown bits from the bottom and sides of the pan. Pour this liquid into the large saucepan.

3. Add the garlic, peppercorns and cloves. Pour in enough water to cover the contents of the saucepan by about 75mm. Bring to the boil, then reduce heat to a simmer and skim off any impurities from the surface. Add the thyme and bay leaf, then simmer the stock for about 4 hours, skimming occasionally.

4. When cooked, strain the stock, allow to cool and refrigerate. You can later degrease the stock by lifting the congealed fat from the surface.

5. If you are making a consommé, which must be served fat-free, lightly draw an ice cube over the surface of the stock, the fat will cling to the cube. Alternatively, blot up any fat with absorbent paper.

2lb 4oz (1kg) veal breast or beef or veal shin meat, cut into 3in (75mm) pieces

4lb 6oz (2kg) veal or beef bones, cracked

2 carrots, chopped

4 stalks celery, chopped

3 onions, chopped

3 unpeeled cloves garlic, crushed

8 black peppercorns

3 cloves

4 sprigs fresh thyme, leaves removed and stalks discarded

1 bay leaf

beef

Vegetable beef soup

SERVES 8

1. In a heavy-based frying pan, brown the meat in the olive oil. Pour off excess fat and oil.

2. Cover with 8 cups cold water and bring to the boil. Add salt and onion, simmer for 2 hours.

3. Add vegetables and barley. Simmer for about 1 hour longer. Remove meat from bone, add back to soup and serve.

4lb 6oz (2kg) beef shanks
2 tablespoons olive oil
1 teaspoon salt
1 small onion, chopped
15oz (450g) canned diced
    tomatoes
6 sprigs parsley
5 carrots, sliced
3½oz (100g) green beans, cut
    diagonally
1 medium potato, diced
1 stalk celery, chopped
¼ cup barley

Balinese egg noodle soup

SERVES 6-8

1. Peel and finely chop the shallots, garlic and ginger. Heat the oil and sauté until these flavourings are softened. Remove one-third of this mixture and reserve for the meatballs.

2. To the remaining mixture, add the carrots and sweet potato and sauté for 5 minutes. Add the shredded cabbage and cook until wilted, about 4 minutes. Add the chicken or vegetable stock and the scallion greens and bring to the boil. Simmer for 10 minutes.

3. Meanwhile, make the meatballs. To the reserved shallot mixture, add the minced meat, cilantro, egg white, cornstarch, salt and pepper to taste. Mix well and form into small balls.

4. To the simmering soup, add the meatballs and allow to boil gently for a further 5 minutes. Add the noodles, pushing them down into the soup, and simmer for a further 2 minutes or until the noodles are just tender.

5. Season with the sweet soy sauce and serve garnished with fried onions and red bell pepper.

SOUP

6 French shallots
2 cloves garlic
1½in (4cm) piece fresh ginger
2 carrots, julienned
1 sweet potato, julienned
5oz (150g) Chinese cabbage,
    shredded
8 cups chicken or vegetable
STOCK
8 scallions (spring onions), green
    parts only, julienned
3½oz (100g) dried egg noodles
1 tablespoon sweet soy sauce
2 onions, sliced and fried until
    crisp
1 red bell pepper (capsicum),
    finely shredded
MEATBALLS
2 tablespoons olive oil
9oz (250g) minced beef
2 teaspoons ground coriander
1 egg white
1 tablespoon cornstarch
    (cornflour)
salt and freshly ground
    black pepper

Brown onion & egg yolk soup

SERVES 6

1¾oz (50g) butter
600g onions, peeled and sliced
8 cups beef stock
¼ cup parsley, chopped
1 teaspoon salt
good pinch of cayenne pepper
nutmeg to taste
3 egg yolks
¼ cup port

1. Melt the butter in a heavy-based saucepan and add the onions when the butter is foaming. Allow the onions to go a dark brown colour without burning. Stir the onions constantly while they are browning.

2. Add the stock and bring to the boil. Boil for 45 minutes and then add the parsley, salt and cayenne pepper and nutmeg. Bring back to the boil and cook for a further 10 minutes.

3. To serve, pour the soup into a tureen and keep hot. Take it to the table with the egg yolks and port wine already mixed in a sauceboat. Pour the egg yolk mixture into the soup while stirring and serve immediately with crusty bread.

Hearty beef & barley soup

SERVES 8

⅓ cup wholewheat flour
1 teaspoon salt
17½oz (500g) lean stewing beef
2 tablespoons olive oil
1 medium onion, chopped
4 large cloves garlic, minced
½ medium carrot, grated
1 stalk celery, chopped
1 large tomato, diced
1 cup barley
5 cups chicken stock
¼ cup basil, chopped
1 bay leaf
salt and freshly ground
    black pepper

1. In a plastic bag, combine flour, salt and meat. Shake vigorously.

2. In a large saucepan, pour in the oil and quickly brown the meat over medium heat. Add onions and garlic and cook until soft, about 3–4 minutes. Add the carrot, celery and tomato and continue cooking for about 5 minutes.

3. Add barley, stock and basil and bring to the boil. Wrap the bay leaf in cheesecloth and add to the pot. Lower heat and allow to simmer until the barley is soft, about 20–25 minutes.

4. Season to taste with the salt and pepper. Remove bay leaf before serving.

Hungarian goulash soup

SERVES 8

1. Heat the olive oil in a saucepan and sauté the onion until golden brown, about 5 minutes. Add the paprika, garlic, caraway seeds and marjoram and cook for 1–2 minutes until the mixture is fragrant.
2. Add the beef, diced tomatoes and tomato paste, and cook until the meat is well coated and is a rich brown colour, about 5 minutes. Add the stock, sugar, salt and pepper and bring to the boil. Simmer for 1 hour. Add the potatoes, carrots and continue cooking for a further 30 minutes.
3. Check seasonings and adjust if necessary. Stir the cornstarch mixture into the soup, mixing well. Allow the soup to thicken for a couple of minutes, then serve in individual bowls.
4. Garnish with sour cream, cucumbers and Frankfurters, if using.

3 tablespoons olive oil
2 medium white onions, sliced
2 tablespoons Hungarian (mild) paprika
2 cloves garlic, minced
2 teaspoons caraway seeds
8 sprigs fresh marjoram, leaves removed and stalks discarded
17½oz (500g) diced beef
14oz (400g) canned diced tomatoes
2 tablespoons tomato paste
6 cups beef stock
2 teaspoons brown sugar
1 teaspoon salt
1 teaspoon pepper
14oz (400g) potatoes, diced
7oz (200g) carrots, diced
1 tablespoon cornstarch (cornflour), mixed with 2 tablespoons cold water
¼ cup sour cream
2 pickled cucumbers, finely diced
3 cooked Frankfurters, finely sliced (optional)

Meatballs in egg & lemon soup

SERVES 4

1. Combine the mince, onion, parsley, rice and 1 egg in a bowl, and mix well with your hands. Season well with salt and pepper. Using one tablespoon of mixture for each meatball, shape mixture into balls. Roll in cornstarch, shaking off any excess.

2. Bring the stock and the butter to the boil, then reduce the heat and place the meatballs in the stock. Cover and simmer for 45 minutes. Allow to cool slightly.

3. Whisk the remaining egg and lemon juice together in a bowl, then add ½ cup of warm stock. Pour this mixture back into the saucepan and heat very gently. Season with salt and pepper before serving.

17½oz (500g) beef mince
1 medium onion, finely chopped
¼ cup parsley, chopped
¼ cup medium-grain rice
2 eggs
salt and freshly ground
　　black pepper
⅓ cup cornstarch (cornflour)
4 cups beef stock
1¾oz (50g) butter
⅓ cup lemon juice

Oxtail & tomato soup

SERVES 6

1 medium oxtail
1 medium onion, chopped
1 large carrot, sliced
1 stalk celery, diced
8 cups beef stock
2 tomatoes, peeled, deseeded
   and chopped
salt and freshly ground
   black pepper
1 sprig rosemary, leaves removed
   and chopped

1. Have the oxtail cut into sections by your butcher and place it in a boiling pot with the onion, carrot, celery and beef stock.

2. Simmer until the meat is cooked and is leaving the bone. Remove from the heat and lift the oxtail out. Reserve the stock. Cool the meat and then remove it from the bone. Dice finely and return it to the reserved stock.

3. Add the tomato, rosemary, salt and pepper. Bring to the boil and cook for 10 minutes. Check the seasoning and serve with crusty bread.

Oxtail soup

SERVES 8

1 oxtail
1 tablespoon seasoned flour
2 tablespoons oil
6 cups beef stock
1 carrot, sliced
1 small turnip, sliced
1 onion, roughly chopped
2 stalks celery, chopped
2–3 bay leaves
salt
pinch of cayenne pepper
juice of 1 lemon
1 teaspoon Worcestershire sauce
3 tablespoons sherry or Madeira

1. Coat oxtail in seasoned flour. Heat oil over a medium heat, add oxtail and cook until brown. Add stock and simmer for 2 hours. Skim off the froth.

2. Place vegetables and bay leaves in the stock and cook for a further 15–20 minutes.

3. Remove meat from bones, return the meat to soup and reheat. Season with salt and cayenne pepper. Stir in lemon juice and Worcestershire sauce. Just before serving, add sherry.

Russian cabbage soup

SERVES 6

1. Melt butter in a large saucepan and sauté beef and bacon over a medium heat until browned.
2. Add half the cabbage and all the remaining ingredients except sour cream and Parmesan. Cover, bring to the boil, and simmer for 1½ hours. Add remaining cabbage and cook for 10–15 minutes or until tender. Stir in cream, sprinkle with Parmesan cheese and serve.

1oz (30g) butter
9oz (250g) beef, diced
4oz (125g) bacon pieces
10½oz (300g) cabbage, finely shredded
2 large tomatoes, peeled and diced
2 onions, diced
1 bay leaf
salt and freshly ground black pepper
4 cups beef stock
⅓ cup sour cream
1½oz (40g) Parmesan cheese, grated

Jewish goulash soup

1. Heat the olive oil and sauté the onion until golden brown, about 5 minutes. Add the paprika, garlic, caraway seeds, lemon zest and oregano and cook for a minute or two. Add the beef and tomato paste, and cook until the meat is well coated and is a rich brown colour, about 5 minutes.

2. Add the stock, sugar, bay leaves, salt and pepper and bring to the boil. Simmer for 1 hour.

3. Add the potatoes and continue cooking for a further 30 minutes. Check seasonings and adjust if necessary. Remove bay leaves. Serve in individual bowls, garnished with sour cream and finely diced cucumbers.

2 tablespoons olive oil
1 medium white onion, sliced
1 tablespoon Hungarian paprika
2 cloves garlic, minced
2 teaspoons caraway seeds
zest of ½ lemon
4 sprigs fresh oregano, leaves
    removed and chopped
17½oz (500g) diced beef
2 tablespoons tomato paste
5 cups beef stock
2 teaspoons brown sugar
2 bay leaves
1 teaspoon salt
1 teaspoon pepper
17½oz (500g) potatoes, peeled
    and diced
2 pickled cucumbers, finely diced
¼ cup sour cream

Lentil soup with frankfurters

SERVES 6

1 cup green lentils, rinsed
2 rashers bacon, diced
1 leek, washed and finely diced
1 large carrot, diced
1 stalk celery, diced
1 tablespoon vegetable oil
1 onion, finely chopped
1 tablespoon all-purpose (plain)
    flour
1 tablespoon vinegar
4 Frankfurters, thinly sliced
1 tablespoon tomato sauce
1 teaspoon salt
¼ teaspoon freshly ground
    black pepper

1. Place lentils in a large saucepan, add water and bring slowly to the boil.

2. Add bacon, leek, carrot and celery, partly cover and allow to simmer for 30 minutes.

3. In a small frying pan, heat the oil, add onion and sauté until golden. Stir in flour, lower the heat and stir until flour turns a light golden colour. Sir in a few spoonfuls of soup stock and mix until smooth and free of lumps. Stir in vinegar then add contents of pan to soup. Cover and simmer for 30 minutes. If soup is thickening more than desired, add a little water.

4. Add sliced Frankfurters, tomato sauce, salt and pepper. Simmer for 5 minutes, taste and adjust seasoning to taste. Serve with rye bread.

chicken

Chicken vegetable soup with cheese sticks

SERVES 6

1. Put the chicken in a pot, add just enough chicken stock to cover it and poach gently for about 10 minutes or until just cooked. Set aside to cool.

2. Heat the oil in a large pot, add the leeks and cook gently for about 2 minutes until soft. Add the carrot, celery and garlic, strain the chicken poaching stock through a fine sieve and add to the vegetables with the rest of the stock. Simmer for 10 minutes. Chop the greens finely, add them to the soup and cook for a further 10 minutes.

3. Tear the chicken breasts into fine shreds and add them to the soup. Stir in the pesto and season with plenty of cracked black pepper.

CHEESE STICKS

1. Preheat the oven to 420°F (220°C). Cut the puff pastry into ¾in (2cm)-thick strips and place on a baking tray lined with baking paper. Sprinkle with the cheese and bake for 20 minutes or until crisp and golden.

2. Serve the soup in wide bowls with cheese sticks.

2 skinless chicken breast fillets
4 cups chicken stock
1 tablespoon canola oil
2 leeks, washed and thinly sliced
2 carrots, diced
2 stalks celery, diced
3 cloves garlic, crushed
6 cups young green leaves
  (watercress, rocket, sorrel,
  baby spinach), washed
3 tablespoons fresh pesto
freshly cracked black pepper
CHEESE STICKS
1 sheet puff pastry, thawed
1½oz (40g) Cheddar cheese,
  finely grated

Chicken & corn soup

SERVES 12

1. Wash chicken and place into a large saucepan with 10 cups water. Bring to the boil and simmer approximately 40 minutes or until chicken is cooked. Remove chicken from pan, set aside to cool. Do not discard chicken stock. While chicken is cooking, prepare other ingredients.

2. Place water chestnuts, onion, bacon and ginger into food processor or blender bowl and process until finely chopped. Remove from bowl.

3. Purée corn niblets in food processor or blender.

4. Remove skin and bones from chicken. Place chicken into processor bowl and process until finely chopped.

5. Take 2 cups of chicken stock from pan and reserve for future use.

6. Add all prepared ingredients with reserved corn liquid to chicken stock.

7. Add green onions to saucepan with sesame oil, salt and pepper. Bring to boil. Mix cornstarch and 1/3 cup water to a smooth paste, add to soup and simmer, stirring, for 3 minutes. Add sherry and soy sauce. Lightly beat egg with a fork, add to soup and stir for 1 minute. Serve.

2lb 12oz (1¼kg) chicken
½ cup water chestnuts, drained
1 small onion, peeled and halved
2 rashers bacon, each rasher cut into quarters, rind removed
¼in (1cm) piece green ginger, peeled
15oz (440g) canned corn niblets, drained, reserving liquid
6 scallions (spring onions), sliced
2 teaspoons sesame oil
salt and freshly ground black pepper
3 tablespoons cornstarch (cornflour)
1 tablespoon sweet sherry
2 teaspoons soy sauce
1 egg

Chicken & leek soup

SERVES 6

2lb 4oz (1kg) boiling chicken
1 onion, chopped
1 carrot, peeled and chopped
pinch saffron
1 stalk celery, chopped
2 leeks, finely sliced
1oz (30g) butter
salt
cayenne pepper
½ cup thickened cream

1. In a large pot, place the chicken, onion, carrot, saffron and celery. Cover the ingredients with water and boil for 1 hour.
2. Remove from the heat and strain off the stock. Reserve the chicken.
3. Sauté the leeks in the butter until soft, add the chicken stock and, heat through. Season with salt and cayenne pepper. Add cream as desired and serve.

Chicken soup with lemon & mint

SERVES 4

1 tablespoon olive oil
17½oz (500g) chicken breast
　fillets, trimmed
8 cups chicken stock
¾ cup medium- or long-grain rice
¼ cup lemon juice
⅓ cup fresh mint, chopped
salt and freshly ground
　black pepper

1.　Heat oil in a large saucepan over
medium heat. Add chicken fillets and cook
for 2 minutes each side or until just light
golden. Add ½ cup stock and simmer over
low heat until chicken is cooked. Remove
and cut into thin slices.

2.　Heat remaining stock in saucepan over
medium heat. Bring to the boil, add rice and
cook for 12 minutes or until cooked. Add
chicken and cook for a further 5 minutes.

3.　Stir in lemon juice, mint and season to
taste with salt and pepper. Serve with crusty
bread.

Hot & sour chicken soup

SERVES 6

1. Brush the chicken strips with 1 tablespoon of peanut oil and grill or pan-fry until the chicken is golden brown and slightly charred, about 3 minutes each side.

2. Heat the remaining tablespoon of peanut oil in a large saucepan and add the garlic, shallots, cilantro leaves and stems, ginger, chillies, lemongrass and lime leaves and toss in the hot oil until fragrant, about 2 minutes. Add the stock and bring to the boil. Simmer for 10 minutes, then add the grilled chicken strips and simmer for a further 10 minutes.

Add the fish sauce and noodles and simmer for a further 2 minutes, or until the noodles are tender. Add the sliced scallions, lime juice and cilantro leaves, remove the lemongrass and serve very hot.

21oz (600g) chicken breast fillets, cut into ¼in- (1cm) thick strips
2 tablespoons peanut oil
4 cloves garlic, minced
2 French shallots, chopped
5 stems of cilantro (coriander), leaves included, chopped
1oz (30g) fresh ginger, bruised
3 small red Thai chillies, minced
3 stalks lemongrass, bruised
6 kaffir lime leaves, finely shredded
8 cups chicken or vegetable stock
3 tablespoons fish sauce
3½oz (100g) cellophane or glass noodles
6 scallions (spring onions), diagonally sliced
juice of 1–2 limes
½ cup cilantro (coriander) leaves

Mulligatawny

1. Melt butter in a saucepan over medium heat. Add onion, ginger and curry powder and cook until onion is tender. Add the flour and coconut and cook for a further 2 minutes. Add the stock, bouquet garni and tomato paste. Bring to the boil and simmer over low heat for 45 minutes.

2. Add the chutney, banana, chicken, lemon juice and seasonings. Heat through, remove bouquet garni and serve sprinkled with boiled rice.

1oz (30g) butter
1 small onion, finely diced
¼in (1cm) piece ginger, grated
1 tablespoon curry powder
1 tablespoon all-purpose (plain) flour
1 tablespoon desiccated coconut
4 cups chicken stock
1 bouquet garni
1 tablespoon tomato paste
1 tablespoon mango chutney
½ small banana, sliced
5oz (150g) cooked chicken breast, diced
juice of ½ lemon
salt and freshly ground black pepper

Thai rice soup with chicken

SERVES 4

½ cup short-grain rice
1 tablespoon vegetable oil
1 large clove garlic,
    finely chopped
1½in (4cm) piece fresh ginger,
    finely grated
9oz (250g) chicken thigh or
    breast fillets, trimmed and
    diced
white pepper
2 tablespoons fish sauce
1 small onion, finely sliced
¼ cup fresh cilantro (coriander),
    chopped
1 scallion (spring onion),
    chopped

1. Place rice in a large saucepan with 8 cups water and bring slowly to the boil. Simmer gently, adding more water as necessary so that mixture becomes a thin porridge consistency.

2. In a wok or large frying pan, heat the oil and stir-fry the garlic and ginger. Add the chicken and season with pepper and fish sauce. Add the onion and stir-fry until chicken is cooked, about 5 minutes. Stir into the rice stock.

3. Just before serving, stir in the cilantro and green onions. Ladle into heated bowls and garnish each with a few extra cilantro leaves, scallion and some sliced red chillies.

Traditional Jewish chicken soup

SERVES 10

SOUP

2 tablespoons vegetable oil
3 large onions, chopped
3 large carrots, chopped
4 stalks celery, chopped
4lb 6oz (2kg) chicken wings,
    frames or chicken pieces
4 bay leaves
6 sprigs parsley
10½oz (300g) piece of beef top
    rib

MATZOH BALLS

2 tablespoons vegetable oil
1 large onion, finely diced
4 large eggs
¼ small bunch chives, chopped
1–1½ cups matzoh meal
salt and freshly ground
    black pepper

1. First, make the soup. Heat the oil in a very large saucepan and add the onions, carrots and celery and sauté in the oil until golden, about 10 minutes. Add the chicken, bay leaves, parsley, top rib and 4 litres of water and bring to the boil. Simmer for 5 hours, skimming the scum off the surface as it becomes visible. After 5 hours, taste the soup and season to taste. Chill the soup overnight. The next day, skim the fat off the surface of the soup then reheat until just warm. Strain the soup into a clean pot, discard the solids.

2. To make the matzoh balls, heat the vegetable oil in a frying pan and add the finely chopped onions. Sauté until the onions are deep golden brown. Remove the pan from the heat and add the eggs, chives, matzoh meal and salt and pepper to taste and mix thoroughly. Allow the mixture to chill for 2 hours. Bring a large pot of salted water to the boil and then shape the matzoh mixture into walnut-size balls and drop them into the boiling water. Simmer for approximately 30 minutes or until tender. Remove with a slotted spoon and set aside.

3. To serve, reheat the soup until scalding then add the matzoh balls to heat them through. Serve 1–2 matzoh balls per person with a bowl of the golden soup and garnish with extra parsley.

Vermicelli & chicken soup

SERVES 6

1. Make stock by boiling all ingredients together with 8 cups water, then simmering for 1 hour. Strain reduced stock and discard the bones and vegetables.

2. Boil chicken chunks in stock for 15 minutes, skimming scum from the surface. Add vermicelli and mushrooms, and cook until vermicelli is done.

3. Season with salt and pepper and serve sprinkled with chopped spring onion.

5oz (150g) chicken breast, cut into chunks
9oz (250g) Chinese mung bean vermicelli
½ cup button mushrooms, sliced
salt
½ teaspoon black or white pepper
1 scallion (spring onion), chopped

STOCK

3 teaspoons fish sauce
1 onion, quartered
3lb 5oz (1½kg) pork bones
17½oz (500g) chicken wings, bones and/or leftover meat scraps
17½oz (500g) of 2 of the following: whole carrot, quartered cauliflower, whole green beans, quarter of a cabbage

Chicken & coconut soup

SERVES 6

1. Place coconut milk and 2 cups water in a saucepan and bring to the boil over a medium heat. Add chicken, galangal or ginger, lemongrass, cilantro (coriander) root and lime leaves and simmer for 6 minutes.

2. Stir in chillies, fish sauce and lemon juice. To serve, ladle into bowls and scatter with cilantro (coriander) leaves.

NOTE

This popular Thai soup is known as tom kha gai. When dining in the traditional Thai manner, soups are not served as a separate course but are eaten with the other dishes and rice.

3 cups coconut milk
17½oz (500g) chicken breast
    fillets, cut into ¼in- (1cm)
    thick strips
1½in (4cm) piece fresh galangal
    or ginger, sliced
2 stalks lemongrass, cut into
    1½in (4cm) pieces
1 fresh cilantro (coriander) root,
    bruised
4 kaffir lime leaves, shredded
3 fresh red chillies, deseeded and
    chopped
2 tablespoons fish sauce
2 tablespoons lemon juice
¼ cup fresh cilantro (coriander)
    leaves

lamb

Chunky lamb soup

1. Melt the butter in a large saucepan over moderate heat. Add lamb cubes, onion, parsley, paprika, saffron and pepper. Cook for 5 minutes, stirring frequently.

2. Add the stock. Drain chickpeas and add them to pan with tomatoes and lemon juice. Bring to the boil, boil for 10 minutes, then cover pan and simmer for 1–1¼ hours.

3. Stir in rice. Cook for 15–20 minutes or until tender. Serve at once, in heated bowls.

1oz (30g) butter
17½oz (500g) lamb fillet, cut into ¾in (2cm) cubes
1 large onion, chopped
¼ cup fresh parsley, chopped
2 teaspoons paprika
1 teaspoon saffron powder
1 teaspoon freshly ground black pepper
6 cups lamb or chicken stock
2oz (60g) chickpeas, soaked overnight in water
17½oz (500g) tomatoes, peeled, deseeded and chopped
4 tablespoons lemon juice
2oz (60g) long-grain rice

Turkish wedding soup

1. Coat the shanks in seasoned flour. Heat oil and half the butter, add shanks and cook until brown. Add 6 cups water, bring to the boil, and skim off the froth.

2. Reduce heat, add the onion, salt and pepper and simmer covered for 2 hours or until the lamb is tender. Allow to cool and refrigerate overnight.

3. Skim off the fat, strain into a saucepan and discard the onion. Remove meat from the shanks. Chop meat and return to the stock.

4. Add egg yolks and lemon juice and cook, without boiling. Melt the remaining butter and stir in paprika and cayenne pepper. Garnish with the paprika mixture and serve.

2lb 4oz (1kg) lamb shanks, bones broken
¼ cup seasoned flour
1 tablespoon oil
2oz (60g) butter
1 onion, grated
salt and freshly ground black pepper
3 egg yolks
¼ cup lemon juice
1½ teaspoons paprika
pinch of cayenne pepper

Lamb shank and vegetable soup

SERVES 6

4 lamb shanks, French trimmed

3 stalks celery, cut into ¼in (1cm) pieces

2 medium carrots, peeled andcut into ¼in (1cm) pieces

1 swede, peeled and cut into ¼in (1cm) cubes

1 parsnip, peeled and cut into ¼in (1cm) cubes

1lb 12oz (800g) canned tomato soup

⅓ cup flat-leaf parsley, coarsely chopped

salt and freshly ground black pepper

1. Combine lamb shanks, celery, carrot, swede, parsnip, tomato soup and 6 cups cold water in a large saucepan over high heat and bring to the boil. Reduce heat to low and simmer, covered, stirring occasionally, for 2¼ hours or until the lamb is tender and falling away from the bone.

2. Remove from heat and stir in parsley. Use tongs to remove the bones. Taste and season with salt and pepper. Ladle soup into bowls and serve with crusty bread.

Lamb shank broth

SERVES 8

1oz (30g) butter
1 large onion, sliced
4 lamb shanks
½ cup barley
3 stalks celery, sliced
2 large carrots, sliced
2 large parsnips, diced
2 tomatoes, diced
1 teaspoon salt
freshly ground black pepper
¼ cup parsley, chopped

1. Melt the butter in a large saucepan. Add the onion and cook over a low heat for 10 minutes. Add the shanks, barley, celery, carrots, parsnips, tomatoes and 12 cups water. Season with salt and pepper. Cover and simmer for 1½–2 hours.

2. Remove the lamb shanks and chop the meat. Return the meat to the soup and discard the bones. Adjust seasoning if necessary.

3. Serve sprinkled with parsley and accompanied with wholemeal crusty bread rolls.

Lamb soup with cheese

SERVES 4

1. Place the lamb in a saucepan. Add the onion, garlic and bay leaves and cover with 4 cups water. Bring to the boil and simmer gently for an hour.

2. Remove the lamb and cut the meat into small pieces – discard the bones, but keep the lamb stock.

3. In a large saucepan, melt the butter and add the flour. Cook for a minute, stirring all the time, then add the milk.

4. Simmer the sauce for 2 minutes, add the cheese, the lamb stock, lamb pieces and vegetables. Simmer gently for 30 minutes, stirring occasionally. Season with salt and pepper to taste.

5. Serve garnished with chopped parsley and accompanied with crusty bread.

1lb 10oz (750g) neck lamb chops on the bone
1 large onion, finely chopped
3 cloves garlic, finely chopped
2 bay leaves
1oz (30g) butter
2 tablespoons all-purpose (plain) flour
1 cup milk
4oz (125g) Cheddar cheese, grated
4 carrots, diced
2 leeks, finely chopped
3 medium potatoes, peeled and diced
salt and freshly ground black pepper
¼ cup fresh parsley, chopped

Lamb soup

1. Heat the butter in a heavy based saucepan and fry the lamb in small quantities until brown on all sides.

2. Put all other ingredients into the saucepan with the lamb and 12 cups water. Bring to the boil, turn down the heat and cook for 2½ hours.

3. Serve with pappadams and boiled rice.

1¾oz (50g) butter
2lb 4oz (1kg) lamb fillet, chopped
4oz (125g) split red lentils, washed
4oz (125g) green lentils, washed
4oz (125g) yellow split peas, soaked overnight
2 onions, chopped
14oz (400g) canned chopped tomatoes
7oz (200g) pumpkin, peeled and chopped
2 potatoes, peeled and chopped
14oz (400g) eggplant, finely chopped
1 teaspoon ground coriander
1 teaspoon ground cumin
1 teaspoon garam masala
½ teaspoon ground turmeric
1 teaspoon chilli powder
4 red chillies, deseeded and chopped
12 fresh mint leaves, chopped
½ cup cilantro (coriander) leaves
1in (25mm) piece of ginger, grated
4 cloves garlic, finely chopped
1oz (30g) shredded coconut
salt and freshly ground black pepper

Libyan lamb & chickpea soup

SERVES 6

1 tablespoon olive oil

1 large brown onion,
  finely chopped

17½oz (500g) stewing lamb,
  finely chopped

7oz (200g) canned chickpeas,
  rinsed and drained

3 tablespoons tomato purée

1 teaspoon ground coriander

1 teaspoon ground turmeric

½ teaspoon chilli powder

½ teaspoon salt

1½ tablespoons dried mint

juice of ½ lemon

6 fresh mint sprigs

1 lemon, cut into wedges

1. Heat the oil in a large casserole or saucepan. Gently fry the onion for a few minutes until pale golden and soft.

2. Add the lamb, chickpeas, tomato purée, spices and salt, cooking for a few more minutes and stirring well.

3. Add 4 cups water to the saucepan – this should cover the mixture – then add 1 cup more if required. If adding extra water, remember that you may need to add a little extra spice and salt to compensate.

4. Cover and simmer over a medium heat for approximately 45–50 minutes or until the lamb is tender. If required, you may add a little extra water again at this point, but remember to adjust the seasoning if you do.

5. Add the dried mint and the lemon juice, return to the heat for a further 3–4 minutes then serve each bowl with a sprig of fresh mint and a lemon wedge on the side.

Smoky lamb & eggplant soup

SERVES 6-8

2lb 4oz (1kg) eggplants
2½oz (80g) ghee or butter
2 large leeks
17½oz (500g) sweet potato,
    peeled and cubed
2 teaspoons ground cumin
2 teaspoons ground cinnamon
4lb 6oz (2kg) lamb shanks
4 cups beef stock
4 sprigs thyme
3 cinnamon sticks
1 cup flat-leaf parsley, chopped

1. Prick the eggplants all over and place them on a grill or barbecue, turning often until charred and deflated. Alternatively, bake at 430°F (220°C) for 1 hour until the eggplants are soft and deflated. Chop the eggplant, discarding any very tough or charred skin.

2. Heat half the ghee or butter in a large saucepan, add the leeks and sauté until golden. Add the chopped eggplant, sweet potato, cumin and ground cinnamon and stir thoroughly while cooking for 5 minutes or until all the ingredients are golden and fragrant. Place this mixture in a bowl and set aside.

3. In the used saucepan, heat the remaining ghee or butter and add the lamb shanks, cooking them over a medium-high heat until they are golden all over. Add the beef stock, thyme, cinnamon sticks and 6 cups water and simmer for 1 hour.

4. Remove the shanks and, to the remaining soup, add the eggplant mixture and half the parsley. Simmer for 10 minutes. Meanwhile, cut all the meat off the lamb shanks and return this meat to the soup. Discard the bones.

5. Remove and discard the cinnamon sticks and thyme sprigs, then reheat the soup until simmering. Season to taste with salt and pepper. Stir well then serve with the remaining parsley and black pepper.

Middle Eastern spinach & meatball soup

SERVES 4

1. Mix together the lamb, minced onion, garlic and lots of salt and pepper, then shape the meat mixture into walnut-size balls and refrigerate for 30 minutes.

2. Heat the olive oil and add the leeks to the saucepan, sautéing until they are golden. Add the turmeric and cinnamon and continue stirring and cooking until the mixture is fragrant, about 2 minutes. Add the split peas and stock and bring to the boil. Simmer for 30 minutes.

3. Add the meatballs to the soup and simmer for 10 minutes. Add the spinach and potato cubes and continue simmering for 10 minutes.

4. Mix the rice flour with a little water and the lemon juice and whisk until smooth, then drizzle this mixture into the soup. Season and simmer for 10 more minutes.

5. Finally, fold through the yoghurt, being careful not to let the soup boil. Heat a little extra oil then fry the shallot slices until crisp and deep golden brown. Garnish the soup with the fried shallots and the finely sliced mint leaves.

9oz (250g) minced lamb
1 large brown onion, finely minced
2 cloves garlic, minced
salt and freshly ground black pepper
2 tablespoons olive oil
2 large leeks, sliced
1 tablespoon ground turmeric
1 tablespoon ground cinnamon
4oz (120g) yellow split peas
6 cups vegetable stock
17½oz (500g) spinach, chopped
14oz (400g) potatoes, peeled and cubed
4 tablespoons rice flour
juice of 2 lemons
3 tablespoons natural yoghurt
4 French shallots, sliced
10 mint leaves, finely sliced

Lamb shank barley soup

SERVES 8

1. Bring the lamb shanks, stock and salt to the boil. Add barley and bring back to the boil.
2. Skim off any froth from the surface, cover and gently simmer over low heat for 2–3 hours. Add vegetables and simmer for a further 30 minutes.
3. Remove the shank bones, chop the meat and return to the soup. Season with salt and pepper, garnish with parsley and serve.

4 lamb shanks, fat removed
6 cups beef stock
1 teaspoon salt
½ cup barley, washed
2 medium onions, finely diced
2 medium carrots, medium diced
2 stalks celery, thinly sliced
1 small turnip, medium diced
freshly ground black pepper
¼ cup parsley, chopped

pork

Broccoli & bacon soup

SERVES 4

1. Heat the oil in a large saucepan and sauté the onion and garlic for 5 minutes until clear. Pour in stock and bring to the boil.

2. Add broccoli and cook for 10 minutes until just tender. Purée in a blender or food processor.

3. Return soup to saucepan. Mix in bacon and milk. Cook for 5 minutes. Season with freshly ground black pepper. Serve garnished with chopped chives.

1 tablespoon olive oil
1 large onion, roughly chopped
2 cloves garlic, chopped
3 cups chicken stock
17½oz (500g) broccoli
3 rashers bacon, rind removed,
    cut into small pieces
1 cup milk
freshly ground black pepper

Asian pork soup

SERVES 4

1. Heat the oil in a large non-stick saucepan over medium heat. Add pork to hot saucepan and cook for 2–3 minutes or until slightly pink in centre.
2. Remove from the saucepan and set aside. Add mushrooms and garlic to saucepan and stir until tender over medium heat.
3. Stir in chicken stock, sherry, soy sauce, ginger, and red pepper. Bring to the boil. Stir in pork, Chinese cabbage, and green onion, heat through and serve.

2 tablespoons olive oil
14oz (400g) pork fillet, cut into thin bite-size pieces
3½oz (100g) shiitake mushrooms, sliced
2 cloves garlic, minced
6 cups chicken stock
2 tablespoons dry sherry
2 tablespoons soy sauce
¾in (2cm) piece ginger, minced
¼ teaspoon red pepper
5oz (150g) Chinese cabbage, thinly sliced
1 scallion (spring onion), thinly sliced

Corn & bacon chowder

SERVES 8

6 rashers bacon, rind removed,
  chopped
1 medium onion, thinly sliced
17½oz (500g) potatoes, peeled
  and medium diced
29½oz (880g) canned creamed
  sweetcorn
3 cups milk
1 sprig thyme, leaves removed
  and stalk discarded
salt and freshly ground
  black pepper
dash of Worcestershire sauce

1. Place bacon in a saucepan and sautè over medium heat until crisp. Remove and drain on absorbent paper.

2. Sautè onion until tender, add potatoes and 5 cups boiling water and cook for a further 10 minutes. Add sweetcorn, milk, thyme and bacon, bring to the boil, season with salt, pepper and Worcestershire sauce. Garnish with extra fresh thyme or parsley.

Heavenly soup with ham

SERVES 4

4 cups chicken stock
1½ tablespoons light soy sauce
1 teaspoon sugar
2 eggs, lightly beaten
1 slice of ham, finely diced
2 scallions (spring onions),
  finely chopped

1. Bring stock to the boil, and add soy sauce and sugar.

2. Just before serving, pour the eggs into the stock, but do not stir. The egg should soon coagulate into egg flowerets. Stir only when the egg has started to set. Garnish with ham and scallions and serve.

Long soup

SERVES 12

1. Place ham, water chestnuts, ginger and bamboo shoots into food processor bowl. Process until finely chopped. Set aside.

2. Finely mince one-third of the cubed pork at a time. Heat oil in a large saucepan, add minced pork and cook for 5 minutes, stirring frequently. Add the cabbage, scallions, ham, water chestnuts, ginger, bamboo shoots, stock, salt, pepper, soy sauce and egg noodles. Bring to boil and simmer for 10 minutes or until noodles are tender. Stir through sherry and serve.

¼ cup water chestnuts, drained
¼in (1cm) cube green ginger
4oz (125g) bamboo shoots, drained
4oz (125g) lean pork, cut into 1in (25mm) cubes
1 tablespoon oil
9oz (250g) cabbage, sliced
5 scallions (spring onions), sliced
2 slices ham
12 cups chicken stock
salt and freshly ground black pepper
¼ cup soy sauce
3oz (90g) thin egg noodles
¼ cup sweet sherry

Pea soup

SERVES 8

1. Wash peas and soak in water overnight. Place peas, water and bones in a saucepan and bring to the boil. Add prepared vegetables and simmer for 1½ hours.
2. Remove bones, purée mixture, and season with salt and pepper. Thicken with flour paste and, stirring continuously, cook for 3 minutes. Garnish with croutons and serve immediately.

9oz (250g) split peas
17½oz (500g) bacon bones
2 carrots, roughly chopped
2 turnips, roughly chopped
2 onions, roughly chopped
4 stalks celery, chopped
salt and freshly ground
    black pepper
1 tablespoon all-purpose (plain)
    flour, mixed with 1 tablespoon
    water

Pork & vegetable soup

SERVES 4

14oz (400g) boneless pork, cut
into ½in (15mm) cubes

2 tablespoons all-purpose (plain)
flour

1 tablespoon vegetable oil

1 medium onion, chopped

2 stalks celery, diced

3 cups chicken stock

½ teaspoon dried marjoram

2 medium potatoes, peeled and
diced

4oz (125g) mushrooms, chopped

½ medium green capsicum,
chopped

2 tablespoons diced pimiento

¼ cup flat-leaf parsley, chopped

1. Place pork and flour in a plastic bag and shake until coated.

2. Heat oil in a large saucepan. Add the pork and brown lightly.

3. Add onion and sauté 2–3 minutes longer. Add celery, stock and marjoram. Bring to the boil. Cover and simmer for 15 minutes.

4. Add potatoes and mushrooms. Bring to the boil again. Cover and simmer for 10 minutes. Stir in green capsicum and pimiento. Simmer for 5 minutes more.

5. Sprinkle with parsley. Ladle into bowls.

Pork, mushroom & corn soup

SERVES 4

7oz (200g) lean pork
4 dried Chinese mushrooms
15oz (425g) canned baby corn
1 tablespoon oil
2 cloves garlic, crushed
½ teaspoon ground black pepper
1 cilantro (coriander) plant,
   roots included, chopped
1 onion, chopped
2 tablespoons fish sauce
½ cup fresh basil, chopped

1. Chop pork and set aside. Soak dried mushrooms in boiling water for 30 minutes. Drain and slice. Drain baby corn and rinse well, then cut into bite-size pieces.
2. Meanwhile, heat oil in a large saucepan, add garlic, pepper, cilantro and onion and fry for 2 minutes. Add chopped pork and fry until pork is golden brown.
3. Add 4 cups water, fish sauce, baby corn and mushrooms and bring to the boil. Lower heat, cover and simmer for 10 minutes. Serve hot, sprinkled with chopped basil leaves.

Southwestern pork soup

1. Heat a small non-stick casserole dish over medium-heat and add oil.

2. Add onion, capsicum, garlic and jalapeño and sauté for 2 minutes.

3. Add pork and cook for 3 minutes. Add stock, chilli powder, cumin, salt, pepper, pinto beans and tomatoes and bring to the boil.

4. Partially cover, reduce heat, and simmer for 6 minutes or until pork is done, stirring occasionally. Remove from heat and stir in cilantro. Serve with avocado.

1 tablespoon olive oil
1 medium onion, chopped
½ green capsicum, chopped
4 large cloves garlic, minced
1 jalapeño pepper, deseeded and minced
17½oz (500g) pork tenderloin, trimmed and cut into bite-size pieces
2 cups chicken stock
2 teaspoons chilli powder
1 teaspoon ground cumin
½ teaspoon salt
¼ teaspoon black pepper
17½oz (500g) canned pinto beans, rinsed and drained
14oz (400g) canned diced tomatoes, undrained
¼ cup fresh cilantro (coriander), chopped
1 avocado, diced

Stone soup

SERVES 4-6

1. Heat the oil in a large saucepan over medium heat. Cook the onion and garlic until soft. Add the bacon and cook for 2 minutes. Add the ham hock or bacon bones, potatoes, carrots, turnips, celery, bay leaves and stock.

2. Bring to the boil, reduce heat to low and simmer covered for 40–45 minutes or until vegetables are tender. If time permits, simmer for 1 hour, as this gives the soup more flavour. Add cabbage and kidney beans and simmer for a further 5 minutes.

3. Remove ham hock or bacon bones and cut the meat into small pieces. Return meat to the saucepan, add parsley and season with salt and pepper. Serve with crusty bread.

1 tablespoon olive oil
1 onion, finely chopped
2 cloves garlic, crushed
7oz (200g) smoked bacon, diced
9oz (250g) smoked ham hock or
    bacon bones
2 potatoes, diced
2 carrots, diced
2 turnips, diced
2 stalks celery, diced
2 bay leaves
6 cups vegetable or chicken stock
5oz (150g) Savoy or green
    cabbage, shredded
14oz (400g) canned red kidney
    beans, drained and rinsed
¼ cup fresh parsley, chopped
salt and freshly ground
    black pepper

Tomato and meatball soup

SERVES 4

1 egg, beaten
1 tablespoon soy sauce
1 tablespoon sherry
½ small onion, chopped
¼in (1cm) piece fresh ginger,
  finely grated
9oz (250g) lean minced pork or
  beef
2 tablespoons cornstarch
  (cornflour)
4 cups beef stock
1 leek, finely sliced
4 firm, ripe tomatoes, peeled,
  deseeded and diced
¼ cup fresh cilantro (coriander),
  chopped

1. Combine the egg, soy sauce, sherry, onion and ginger in a bowl, add the meat and cornstarch, then mix well and set aside.
2. Place the stock in a large saucepan, add the leek and tomatoes and bring to the boil. Boil for 2–3 minutes, then lower the heat.
3. Drop rounded teaspoonfuls of the meat mixture into the soup, cover and gently simmer for 3–4 minutes or until meatballs are cooked. Serve sprinkled with cilantro.

NOTE
The meatballs for this soup are also delicious made with thyme, rosemary or parsley. Or you might like to try a mixture of herbs for something different.

seafood

Hot & sour soup

SERVES 6

1. Place the shallots, chillies, lime leaves, ginger and stock in a saucepan and bring to the boil over a high heat. Reduce the heat and simmer for 3 minutes.

2. Add the fish, prawns, mussels and mushrooms and cook for 3–5 minutes or until the fish and seafood are cooked. Discard any mussels that do not open after 5 minutes of cooking. Stir in the lime juice and fish sauce. To serve, ladle the soup into bowls, scatter with cilantro leaves and accompany with lime wedges.

NOTE
Straw mushrooms are one of the most popular mushrooms used in Asian cooking and in the West are readily available canned. Oyster mushrooms are also known as abalone mushrooms and range in colour from white to grey to pale pink. Their shape is similar to that of an oyster shell and they have a delicate flavour. Oyster mushrooms should not be eaten raw as some people are allergic to them in the uncooked state.

4 French shallots, sliced

2 fresh green chillies, chopped

6 kaffir lime leaves

4 slices fresh ginger

8 cups fish, chicken or vegetable stock

9oz (250g) firm fish fillets, cut into chunks

12 medium shrimp (prawns), shelled and deveined, tails left intact

12 mussels, scrubbed and beards removed

4oz (125g) oyster or straw mushrooms

3 tablespoons lime juice

2 tablespoons fish sauce

Clam chowder

1. Melt ½oz (15g) of butter in pan, add bacon and vegetables and cook gently until soft.

2. Add 1¼ cups water and potatoes to vegetables. Simmer until vegetables are tender, approximately 15–20 minutes.

3. Add clams to vegetables and remove the pan from the heat.

4. Melt remaining butter in pan, stir in the flour and cook for 1 minute. Remove from heat and gradually stir in milk.

5. Return soup to heat and add milk mixture. Cook until soup boils and thickens, stirring constantly. Season with salt and pepper, stir through brandy and serve.

1½oz (45g) butter
3 rashers bacon, chopped
1 onion, chopped
1 stalk celery, chopped
1 carrot, chopped
1 potato, peeled and chopped
10oz (280g) canned clams,
    drained and chopped
3 tablespoons all-purpose (plain)
    flour
2½ cups milk
salt and freshly ground
    black pepper
1 tablespoon brandy

Corn & smoked fish soup

SERVES 8

10½oz (300g) smoked fish
8 cups fish stock
4 cobs of corn
salt
cayenne pepper
4 egg yolks
1 cup thickened cream
8 sprigs of dill

1. Poach the smoked fish in the fish stock for 5 minutes. You can add some white wine if you so desire.

2. Remove the fish from the stock and cool. Strip the corn husks then cut the corn kernels from the cob. Place the kernels into the stock and boil until they are tender.

3. Blend or process the stock with the kernels. Return to the pot and season with salt and cayenne pepper. Flake the fish, add to the soup and bring to the boil.

4. In a separate bowl, mix the egg yolks and the cream. Remove the soup from the heat and allow to cool a little. Add the egg yolks and cream, stirring all the time.

5. When ready to serve, bring up to a near boil. In no circumstances allow the soup to boil or it will curdle. Serve garnished with a sprig of dill.

Curried fish soup

SERVES 8

2oz (60g) butter
1 small leek, washed and thinly
    sliced
1 medium carrot, thinly sliced
1 small onion, chopped
1 tablespoon curry powder
1 tomato, peeled, seeds removed
    and chopped
2 cups fish stock
1 large potato, peeled and diced
1 teaspoon brown sugar
½ teaspoon salt
9oz (250g) fish fillets, cut into
    1in (25mm) pieces
salt and freshly ground
    black pepper
1 cup thickened cream
¼ cup parsley, chopped

1. Heat butter in a saucepan and sauté leek, carrot and onion over a low heat for 5 minutes or until the vegetables are tender.
2. Stir in curry powder and cook for 2 minutes. Add tomato and cook for 5 minutes. Stir in stock, potato, sugar and salt and bring to the boil. Reduce the heat and simmer for 15 minutes.
3. Add fish and seasonings and simmer for a further 10 minutes. Stir through cream and reheat without boiling. Sprinkle with parsley and serve.

Hot & sour fish soup

1. Remove head, fins and tail from fish and cut into 8–10 large pieces. Combine fish, nuoc cham, pepper and spring onion, allow to marinate for 15 minutes.

2. Place 6 cups water in a large saucepan and bring to the boil. Add the fish with its marinade and lemongrass. Reduce heat and simmer for 20 minutes.

3. Meanwhile, combine tamarind pulp and ¾ cup boiling water and allow to soak for 15 minutes. Strain mixture through a fine sieve and discard pulp.

4. Add the tamarind liquid, sugar, bamboo shoots, pineapple and tomatoes to the pan. Simmer for 4–5 minutes until fish is tender. Remove lemongrass.

5. Divide bean sprouts amongst serving bowls and spoon hot soup over. Sprinkle with fresh herbs and deep-fried shallots. Serve with lime wedges and sliced chilli on the side.

2lb 4oz (1kg) firm-fleshed fish
1½ tablespoons nuoc cham dipping sauce
¼ teaspoon white pepper
1 scallion (spring onion), chopped
2 stalks lemongrass, bruised
2oz (55g) tamarind pulp
1 tablespoon sugar
9oz (250g) canned sliced bamboo shoots
¾oz (22g) canned sliced pineapple
2 tomatoes, cut into wedges
1 cup bean sprouts
¼ cup mixed fresh Vietnamese herbs such as cilantro (coriander), bitter herb, Asian basil
deep-fried French shallots

Mussel & shrimp soup

SERVES 6

1. Scrub and remove beards from mussels. Soak in clean water for at least 3 hours before use. Peel prawns, place the heads and shells into a boiling pot. Reserve the peeled shrimp for another meal or deep freeze for another occasion.

2. Add the onion, celery, carrot, parsley, fish stock and white wine to the pot. Bring to the boil and then simmer for 45 minutes. Strain the prawn stock.

3. Place the mussels in a suitable size pot, pour in the stock and add the shallots. Boil for 20 minutes. If you need more liquid, add some white wine. Before serving, add the cream and check seasoning. Serve with fresh crusty bread.

2lb 4oz (1kg) fresh mussels
17½oz (500g) cooked king
  shrimp (prawns)
1 large onion, chopped
2 stalks celery, chopped
2 large carrots, chopped
¼ cup parsley, chopped
8 cups fish stock
2 cups white wine
3 French shallots, chopped
1¼ cups thickened cream
salt and freshly ground
  black pepper

Shrimp & pasta soup

SERVES 6

3lb 5oz (1½kg) cooked shrimp (prawns)
1 small onion, chopped
1 stalk celery, chopped
1 small carrot, chopped
10½oz (300g) pasta of choice
2 tablespoons olive oil
4 large cloves garlic, chopped
4 sprigs fresh oregano, leaves removed and chopped
1 large sprig basil, chopped
14oz (400g) canned chopped tomatoes
2 tablespoons tomato paste
1 teaspoon salt
1 teaspoon freshly ground black pepper
½ cup dry vermouth

1. Peel the shrimp, place the heads and shells into a boiling pot, add the onion, celery and carrot. Cover with 6 cups water and boil for 20 minutes, then strain. Reserve the stock and make sure you push all the juice from the heads with the back of a wooden spoon. Discard the solids.

2. Bring a large saucepan of salted water to the boil, add the pasta and cook for 8 minutes or until just firm in the centre (al dente). Drain, set aside and keep warm.

3. In a saucepan, heat the oil, add all remaining ingredients except the prawns and cook for 5 minutes. Add the stock and boil for a further 15 minutes. Reduce the heat, add the prawns and cook for 3 minutes.

4. Reheat the pasta by pan frying or running under hot water. Divide between six soup bowls and ladle the soup into the bowls. Serve with crusty bread.

Seafood bisque

SERVES 8

3oz (90g) butter
1 small onion, diced
1 clove garlic, crushed
1 small carrot, diced
1 stalk celery, sliced
3 cups fish stock
2 tablespoons lemon juice
1 bay leaf
1 sprig thyme, leaves removed
   and stalks discarded
¼ teaspoon Tabasco sauce
½ teaspoon Worcestershire sauce
1 cup thickened cream
2lb 4oz (1kg) seafood, finely
   diced
½ cup dry white wine
1 lemon, thinly sliced
¼ cup parsley, chopped

1. Melt butter and sauté onion and garlic for 5 minutes. Add carrot and celery and cook for a further 3 minutes.

2. Combine the fish stock, lemon juice, bay leaf, thyme, Tabasco and Worcestershire sauce, add to the pot and simmer for 30 minutes or until vegetables are tender.

3. Remove bay leaf, purée mixture, add cream, seafood and wine and reheat without boiling. Garnish with lemon and parsley and serve.

Mussel soup in roasted tomato sauce

SERVES 6

1. Preheat the oven to 350°F (180°C). Wash mussels under water, scrub the shells with a scourer, and remove their beards. Discard any mussels that are open.

2. Place halved fresh tomatoes on a baking tray, drizzle with olive oil, sprinkle with salt and roast in the oven for 20 minutes.

3. Heat a little oil in a saucepan and sauté the garlic and the onion until soft. Add the white wine and cook for 2 minutes. Add the roasted tomatoes, canned tomatoes, tomato paste, stock and chopped oregano. Simmer for 5–10 minutes. Season with salt and pepper. Add mussels, cover, and cook for a further 5 minutes, until mussels have opened. Discard any that do not open.

4. Serve with crusty Italian bread.

3lb 5oz (1½kg) mussels
14oz (400g) fresh tomatoes, halved
⅓ cup olive oil
4 cloves garlic, crushed
1 brown onion, chopped
3½fl oz (100ml) white wine
14oz (400g) canned peeled tomatoes
¼ cup tomato paste
3½fl oz (100ml) fish stock
10 sprigs fresh oregano, leaves removed and chopped
salt and freshly ground black pepper

Seafood dumpling soup

SERVES 8

1. Heat the oil in a frying pan, add the onion and cook for 5 minutes. Place fish into a mixing bowl and add the onion, anchovy sauce, egg, salt and pepper. Mix well, mould into balls and set to one side.

2. Bring the fish stock to the boil and then simmer. Add the moulded fish balls to this stock. Simmer for 20 minutes.

3. Serve in a tureen, or in individual bowls, sprinkled with the green onion tops.

1 tablespoon olive oil
2 onions, finely chopped
1lb 10oz (750g) minced white-fleshed fish
1 tablespoon anchovy sauce
1 egg, lightly beaten
½ teaspoon salt
½ teaspoon freshly ground black pepper
8 cups fish stock
2 green onion tops, chopped

vegetable

Carrot, lentil & pasta soup

SERVES 4

3½oz (100g) cresti di gallo pasta
1 tablespoon salt
1 tablespoon olive oil
1 carrot, roughly chopped
2 small onions, chopped
2 cloves garlic, crushed
½ tablespoon garam masala
7oz (200g) yellow lentils
8 cups vegetable stock
2 tablespoons chopped fresh
    cilantro (coriander)

1. Place the pasta in lots of boiling water in a large saucepan with salt. Cook for 8 minutes or until just firm in the centre (al dente). Drain, set aside and keep warm.

2. Heat oil in a saucepan over a medium heat, add carrot, onions and garlic and cook, stirring occasionally, for 10 minutes or until vegetables are soft. Add garam masala and cook, stirring, for 1 minute longer.

3. Add lentils and stock to pan and bring to the boil. Reduce heat and simmer, stirring occasionally, for 30–40 minutes or until lentils are cooked. Cool slightly.

4. Purée the soup mixture, in batches, in a food processor or blender. Return the purée to a clean saucepan, add the pasta and cook over a low heat, stirring, for 5 minutes or until soup is hot. Stir in cilantro and serve immediately.

NOTE

Cresti di gallo or 'cock's crests' is so named because it resembles a cock's comb. About 1in (3cm) long, it's slightly curved, with a curly outer rib along the back. Any small pasta shape suitable for soups, such as elbow (short-cut) pasta or macaroni can be substituted.

Borscht

1. Peel and slice 3 of the beetroots. Cook in the stock with onion and bouquet garni until quite tender. Cook the remaining beetroot, without peeling, in boiling water until tender. Allow to cool, peel and grate or cut into julienne strips.

2. Remove herbs and onion and purée cooked beetroot. Add sugar, lemon juice, salt and the grated beetroot to the purée. Chill thoroughly. Garnish with a spoonful of sour cream and serve.

4 medium beetroots
4 cups chicken stock
1 onion, peeled and studded with
    4 cloves
1 bouquet garni
1 tablespoon sugar
1 tablespoon lemon juice
salt
¼ cup sour cream

Provençal-style soup with onion pesto

SERVES 4-6

1. For the soup, heat the oil in a large heavy-based saucepan, then add the onion, potato, carrot and yellow capsicum. Cook uncovered for 5 minutes over a medium heat, stirring occasionally, until the vegetables just start to brown.

2. Add the stock, celery and courgette and bring to the boil. Cover and simmer for 10 minutes or until the vegetables are tender. Stir in the tomatoes, tomato purée and season generously. Simmer uncovered for 10 minutes.

3. Meanwhile, make the pesto. Place the scallions, Parmesan and oil in a food processor and process together to a fairly smooth paste. Ladle the soup into bowls and top with a spoonful of the pesto.

2 tablespoons extra virgin olive oil
1 onion, chopped
1 medium potato, peeled and chopped
1 carrot, chopped
1 yellow capsicum, deseeded and chopped
17½fl oz (500ml) vegetable stock
2 stalks celery, chopped
2 courgette (zucchini), chopped
14oz (400g) canned chopped tomatoes
1 tablespoon tomato purée
sea salt and freshly ground black pepper

ONION PESTO

6 scallions (spring onions), roughly chopped
1¾oz (50g) Parmesan, grated
4 tablespoons extra virgin olive oil

Brussels sprout & leek soup

SERVES 6

14oz (400g) Brussels sprouts,
   trimmed
7oz (200g) white leek, washed
   and trimmed
6 cups vegetable stock
1 cup milk
1¾oz (50g) vermicelli, broken
2 sprigs chervil, chopped

1. Cut the sprouts into quarters or even more if they are large. Slice the leeks very finely, crosswise. Place the two ingredients into a boiling pot and pour in the stock. Bring to the boil and cook until the sprouts are tender.

2. Add the milk and vermicelli and simmer for as long as it takes to cook the vermicelli.

3. A few minutes before you are to serve, add the chervil. Serve hot with hot wholemeal crusty bread and butter.

Cheese & onion soup

SERVES 6

2oz (60g) butter
3 medium onions, finely diced
3 tablespoons all-purpose (plain)
  flour
salt and freshly ground black
  pepper
½ teaspoon paprika
¼ teaspoon sage
pinch of cayenne pepper
3 cups milk
1 cup thickened cream
160g (5½oz) Cheddar cheese,
  grated
½ teaspoon Worcestershire sauce
3 drops Tabasco sauce
⅓ cup whipped cream
½ small bunch chives, chopped

1. Melt butter in a saucepan over a medium heat, add onions and sauté until tender. Add flour, spices and seasonings and cook for 3 minutes.
2. Gradually add milk and cream and cook, stirring continuously over a low heat until thick and smooth. Add cheese and stir until melted. Season with Worcestershire sauce and Tabasco.
3. Garnish with cream, sprinkle with chives and serve.

Cream of cauliflower soup

SERVES 8

1. Combine the cauliflower, onions, stock and milk in a large boiling pot. Cook until the cauliflower is broken down. Remove from heat.

2. Blend the cauliflower and liquid, then return to the pot.

3. Season with salt and cayenne pepper, then add the cream. Reheat and serve garnished with chopped parsley.

1lb 10oz (750g) cauliflower florets
7oz (200g) onions, chopped
6 cups chicken stock
6 cups milk
2 teaspoons salt
¼ teaspoon cayenne pepper
½ cup thickened cream
¼ cup parsley, chopped

Cream of vegetable soup

SERVES 6

1. Melt the butter in a saucepan, add vegetables and cook for 10 minutes over medium heat.
2. Add stock and seasonings and simmer over low heat until vegetables are tender. Purée mixture.
3. Stir in cream and reheat without boiling. Garnish with parsley and serve immediately.

2oz (60g) butter
1lb 10oz (750g) prepared
  vegetables (see below)
2 cups chicken stock
salt and freshly ground black
  pepper
½ cup thickened cream
¼ cup parsley, chopped

PUMPKIN AND LEEK
17½oz (500g) pumpkin, peeled
  and chopped
2 leeks, thinly sliced
¼ cup dry sherry

VARIATIONS
1lb 10oz (750g) carrots, peeled
  and roughly chopped,
  ½ teaspoon allspice OR
1lb 10oz (750g) broccoli, divided
  into florets, ½ teaspoon
  nutmeg OR
1lb 10oz (750g) courgette
  (zucchini), sliced, ¼ teaspoon
  basil OR
1lb 10oz (750g) asparagus, ends
  broken off, stems cut in half OR
1lb 10oz (750g) mushrooms,
  washed and sliced, ½ teaspoon
  oregano, garnish with thinly
  sliced mushrooms

Tomato soup

SERVES 4

1lb 10oz (750g) ripe tomatoes, chopped

1 potato, peeled and chopped

1 small onion, chopped

1 sprig fresh basil

1 teaspoon sugar

2 tablespoons tomato paste

salt and freshly ground black pepper

1 cup vegetable stock

¼ cup thickened cream

¼ cup parsley, finely chopped

1. Place all ingredients except parsley and cream into a saucepan with the stock. Bring to the boil and simmer, covered, for 20 minutes.

2. Serve soup with a swirl of cream and sprinkle with chopped parsley.

Pumpkin soup

SERVES 6

3lb 5oz (1½kg) pumpkin, peeled
    and cut into large cubes
2 tomatoes, chopped
1 large onion, chopped
5 cups vegetable stock
pinch of salt
pinch of cayenne pepper
⅔ cup thickened cream
¼ cup parsley, finely chopped

1. Combine pumpkin, tomato and onions with the stock in a pan. Simmer gently until pumpkin is tender, approximately 20 minutes.
2. Purée pumpkin mixture. Return to pan, add salt, cayenne pepper and cream and reheat gently.
3. Serve sprinkled with parsley.

Minestrone

1. Heat the oil in a saucepan and cook the onion and garlic for 5 minutes until onion is tender. Add the potatoes and cook for a further 5 minutes. Repeat with the carrots, celery and courgette.

2. Add the beef stock, tomatoes and cheese rind, bring to the boil and simmer covered for 1 hour. If the soup becomes too thick, add more stock.

3. Add the chopped parsley and cannellini beans, and heat for a further 10 minutes.

4. To serve, remove the cheese rind, season with salt and black pepper, and serve with crusty bread.

⅓ cup olive oil
1 medium brown onion, sliced
1 clove garlic, crushed
9oz (250g) potatoes, peeled and chopped
5oz (150g) carrots, thinly sliced
4oz (125g) celery, thinly sliced
5oz (150g) courgette (zucchini), sliced
4 cups vegetable stock
14oz (400g) canned Roma tomatoes
rind from piece of Parmesan cheese
¼ cup parsley, chopped
14oz (400g) canned cannellini beans
salt and freshly ground black pepper

Spring cream soup

SERVES 8

1. In a large saucepan, melt butter over a low heat. Add vegetables and, stirring occasionally, cook gently until leek is transparent. Add 2 cups water, cover and simmer gently until vegetables are tender. Purée.

2. Combine the egg yolks, Parmesan and cream. Gradually stir egg mixture into soup and heat gently over a low heat without boiling. Garnish with parsley and serve.

3oz (90g) butter
½ head celery, chopped
1 leek, sliced
2 carrots, peeled and chopped
2 egg yolks
⅔oz (20g) Parmesan cheese, grated
1 cup thickened cream
¼ cup parsley, chopped

Watercress & potato soup

SERVES 4

1 medium bunch watercress,
  coarsely chopped
2lb 4oz (1kg) potatoes, peeled
  and roughly chopped
4 cups milk
1¼ cups vegetable stock
salt and freshly ground black
  pepper
chopped fennel leaves
croutons and sour cream, for
  garnish

1. Simmer the potatoes in the milk and stock. Add the watercress when the potatoes are nearly cooked, then cook for a further 10 minutes.

2. Purée the ingredients in a blender or food processor. Season with salt and pepper, and chill completely. Serve with the chopped fennel or dill leaves. Garnish with croutons and sour cream.

cold

Gazpacho

1. Soak bread in a little water, and squeeze it out before using (the bread helps to thicken the soup and give it a nice consistency).

2. Blend all vegetables and garlic in a blender or food processor, and push through a sieve into a bowl. Use the blender again to beat bread, oil and vinegar together. Add some of the tomatoes, the cumin seeds and salt to taste. Add a little water and mix into the bowl with the soup. Add a few ice cubes and leave to become cold. You can add more water if necessary.

NOTE

Traditionally this soup was made by crushing the ingredients with a mortar and pestle and then adding cold water. Gazpacho traditionally should be served in wooden bowls and eaten with a wooden spoon. You can make large quantities of gazpacho as it keeps well.

2 slices of stale bread
4lb 6oz (2kg) tomatoes, roughly
    chopped
1 cucumber, peeled and chopped
1 green capsicum, deseeded and
    chopped
1 small onion, chopped
2 cloves garlic, chopped
5 tablespoons olive oil
1–2 tablespoons wine vinegar
1 teaspoon cumin seeds or
    ground cumin

Chilled apricot soup

SERVES 6

1. Combine all ingredients except mint and mix well.
2. Place into a glass bowl and refrigerate for 2 hours. Serve chilled, garnished with mint leaves.

1lb 12oz (800g) canned apricot
  halves, puréed
juice of 1 lemon
juice of 1 orange
2 cups white wine
pinch of nutmeg
¼ cup mint leaves

Chilled asparagus soup

SERVES 6

10½oz (300g) very green
  asparagus spears
4 cups chicken stock
1½oz (40g) butter
1½oz (40g) all-purpose (plain)
  flour
2 cups heated milk
½ cup thickened cream
½oz (15g) Parmesan cheese

1. Remove the woody end from the spears. Place the asparagus in a saucepan and cover with chicken stock. Bring to the boil and cook for 10 minutes.

2. Remove the asparagus and chop off and reserve some of the tips for garnish. Purée the asparagus and then strain. Reserve the strained pulp. Reduce the chicken stock to a quarter by boiling at high heat.

3. In a separate saucepan, melt the butter and add the flour. Combine and remove from the heat after 2 minutes. Add the milk and stir constantly to ensure there are no lumps.

4. Add the reduced chicken stock and asparagus pulp. Stir well and return to the heat. Stir frequently for 10 minutes.

5. Add the cream and the cheese. Season with salt and pepper if necessary. Chill thoroughly and if the colour is a little insipid, add some green colouring. Garnish with reserved asparagus tips.

Chilled dill soup

1. Place stock, onion, courgette, potato and cumin in a large saucepan and bring to the boil. Reduce heat and simmer for 20 minutes or until potatoes are tender. Remove saucepan from heat and set aside to cool slightly.

2. Place soup mixture in a food processor or blender and process until smooth. Transfer soup to a large bowl, stir in sour cream and dill, then cover and chill for 3 hours before serving. Ladle soup into chilled bowls and garnish with dill sprigs.

2 cups vegetable stock
1 large onion, chopped
4 courgette (zucchini), chopped
1 large potato, chopped
½ teaspoon ground cumin
1 cup sour cream
2 tablespoons chopped fresh dill
sprigs fresh dill

Chilled yoghurt soup

SERVES 4-6

1. Peel and grate the cucumber.
2. Combine the cream, yoghurt and vinegars, and whisk lightly, until smooth. Stir in the cucumber, mint, garlic and seasoning. Cover and chill for three hours.
3. Stir and taste for seasoning before serving chilled. Garnish with a slice of cucumber, a sprig of mint and cracked pepper.

1 large telegraph cucumber
1 cup thickened cream
7fl oz (200ml) natural yoghurt
2 tablespoons white wine vinegar
1 tablespoon balsamic vinegar
¼ cup fresh mint, chopped
1 clove garlic, crushed
salt and freshly ground
  black pepper

Iced tomato soup

SERVES 8

3 slices bread, crusts removed

2lb 4oz (1kg) tomatoes, peeled, deseeded and chopped

1 cucumber, peeled, deseeded and chopped

½ onion, chopped

2 cloves garlic, crushed

½ green capsicum, deseeded and chopped

1 teaspoon salt

1 teaspoon ground cumin

2 tablespoons olive oil

2 tablespoons wine vinegar

GARNISH

1 red or green capsicum, diced

1 small cucumber, diced

1 onion, finely chopped

2 hard-boiled eggs, chopped

croutons

1. Place all ingredients in a large bowl and allow to stand for 30 minutes to soften bread and blend flavours.

2. Purée one-third of the mixture at a time in an electric blender or food processor. Pour back into a bowl and thin down to desired consistency with 2–3 cups iced water.

3. Cover and chill well. Adjust seasoning to taste. Serve in chilled bowls or in a large bowl over ice.

4. Place garnish ingredients in separate bowls and allow each diner to add garnish to their own soup.

Peach cooler

SERVES 8

5 very ripe peaches, peeled,
    stoned and roughly chopped
juice of 1 lemon
1 teaspoon caster sugar
24fl oz (750ml) dry white wine
1 small bay leaf
1 clove
1 small piece of cinnamon stick
pinch of salt
½ cup whipped cream
1 teaspoon ground cinnamon

1. Purée the peaches with the lemon juice and sugar. Add the wine, bay leaf, clove, cinnamon stick and salt and bring to the boil over a low heat.

2. Chill thoroughly and strain before serving. Garnish with a spoonful of cream, sprinkle with ground cinnamon and serve.

Pumpkin vichyssoise

SERVES 6

1. Place pumpkin, leek, and stock in a boiling pot and place over a high heat. Boil until the pumpkin has broken down.
2. Remove from the heat and add the salt, cayenne pepper and paprika. Blend or process to a very fine consistency, check seasoning.
3. Chill for 2–3 hours before service.
4. To serve, add cream and garnish with chopped chives.

17½oz (500g) peeled, deseeded butternut pumpkin
9oz (250g) leek, chopped and washed
8 cups chicken stock
1 teaspoon salt
¼ teaspoon cayenne pepper
½ teaspoon paprika
½ cup thickened cream
¼ small bunch chives, chopped

Vichyssoise

SERVES 4

2oz (60g) butter
2 leeks, washed and thinly sliced
1 medium onion, thinly sliced
17½oz (500g) potatoes, peeled
   and sliced
3 cups chicken stock
salt and freshly ground
   black pepper
¾ cup thickened cream
¼ small bunch chives, chopped

1. Melt butter in a saucepan, add leeks and onion and sauté until tender without browning. Add potatoes, stock and seasonings and simmer until soft. Purée.

2. Chill for 2–3 hours. Adjust seasonings, stir in the cream and serve in chilled bowls garnished with chopped chives.

Summer chill

1. Peel the cucumbers, reserving the peel. Purée cucumber flesh, apple and sufficient cucumber peel to give a pale green colour. Add remaining ingredients and mix well. Chill with ice block, garnish with extra sliced apple and cucumber and serve immediately.

2 cucumbers
2 green apples, peeled and cored
2 tablespoon lemon juice
1 cup dry white wine
1 teaspoon sugar

Index

Published in 2013 by
New Holland Publishers
London • Sydney • Cape Town • Auckland

Garfield House 86–88 Edgware Road London W2 2EA United Kingdom
1/66 Gibbes Street Chatswood NSW 2067 Australia
Wembley Square First Floor Solan Road Gardens Cape Town 8001 South Africa
218 Lake Road Northcote Auckland New Zealand

www.newhollandpublishers.com

A catalogue record of this book is available at the British Library and the National Library of
Australia.

ISBN: 9781742573816

Publisher: Fiona Schultz
Design: Lorena Susak
Production director: Olga Dementiev
Printer: Toppan Leefung Printing Ltd (China)

10 9 8 7 6 5 4 3 2 1

Texture: Shutterstock

Follow New Holland Publishers on
Facebook: www.facebook.com/NewHollandPublishers